The Let's Talk Library™

Let's Talk About Having Lyme Disease

Elizabeth Weitzman

The Rosen Publishing Group's
PowerKids Press™
New York

Published in 1997 by The Rosen Publishing Group, Inc.
29 East 21st Street, New York, NY 10010

First Edition

Book Design: Erin McKenna

Photo Illustrations: Front cover by Carrie Ann Grippo; p. 4 © Eric R. Berndt/MIDWESTOCK; pp. 8, 11, 12, 15, 19, 20 by Carrie Ann Grippo; p. 7 © 1989 M. Peres/Custom Medical Stock; p. 16 © 1992 CMSP/Custom Medical Stock.

Weitzman, Elizabeth.
    Let's talk about having lyme disease / Elizabeth Weitzman.
        p.   cm. — (The Let's talk library)
    Includes index.
    Summary: Discusses what Lyme disease is, how one gets it, and what to do about it.
    ISBN 0-8239-5029-8 (lib.bdg.)
    1. Lyme disease—Juvenile literature. [1. Lyme disease. 2. Diseases.] I. Title. II. Series.
RC155.5W45 1996
616.9'2—dc20   96-47210
                                                  CIP
                                                      AC

Manufactured in the United States of America

Contents

1   Jeffrey   5

2   Ticks and Lyme Disease   6

3   Ticks Aren't Picky   9

4   Removing a Tick   10

5   Protect Yourself!   13

6   Ticks Live in the Country   14

7   The Signs of Lyme Disease   17

8   If You Feel Sick   18

9   Your Doctor Can Help You   21

10   Know the Facts   22

   Glossary   23

   Index   24

Jeffrey

The summer Jeffrey turned eight years old, his family went camping. They hiked, swam, and went fishing. Jeffrey thought it was the best week of the whole year. But one month after the trip, he noticed a **rash** (RASH) on his leg. And a few weeks after that, he started to feel sick. He thought he was getting the flu.

But Jeffrey didn't have the flu. He had **Lyme disease** (LIME diz-EEZ).

◄ Fishing or camping can be fun, but it's important to be careful.

Ticks and Lyme Disease

Lyme disease is an illness that is spread by the bites of ticks that have the Lyme disease **germ** (JERM) in their bodies. Ticks are tiny animals that look a lot like spiders. They usually live in very grassy or woodsy areas. They attach themselves to animals, such as deer or mice. Then they drink a little bit of that animal's blood for food. The ticks only take a drop of blood, but it's enough to last them for months.

Ticks live off the blood of other animals. ▶

Ticks Aren't Picky

Ticks can't fly or move quickly, but they can jump. They can only bite animals that live or walk in the grass or woods. Although they like deer and mice the best, they're not very picky. They attach themselves to dogs, cats, and even people. A tick bite doesn't hurt. In fact, if you get bitten you won't even know it unless you see the tick on you. If you ever do find a tick on your body, ask an adult to remove it right away.

◀ Ticks will attach themselves to animals or people.

Removing a Tick

Many ticks don't have the Lyme disease germ living inside of them. But you won't know whether a tick has Lyme disease just by looking at it. That's why you have to get a tick off your skin as soon as you see one. An adult can do this by carefully pulling out the tick with **tweezers** (TWEE-zerz). You should both check to see that there's nothing left in your skin. Then she can clean the area carefully. Keep the tick in a jar in case your doctor wants to see it.

It's important to clean the area on your skin before removing a tick. ▶

Protect Yourself!

If you're going to be in a grassy area that might have animals nearby, you will have to protect yourself against ticks. Tuck your pants into your socks. You may also want to wear a long-sleeved shirt. If you wear light-colored clothes, it will be easier to see if any ticks have tried to attach themselves to you.

Protect your pets, too. Ask your parents to put a tick collar on your dog or cat.

◀ Don't forget to protect yourself before you go into a grassy area.

Ticks Live in the Country

Because ticks live in the grass and on animals, Lyme disease is much more common in the country than in the city. If there are many deer or raccoons in a certain area, there may also be many ticks that carry the disease. This means there could be several people with the illness in one town. But the only way to get Lyme disease is from a tick. You cannot catch it from another person.

There are more ticks in grassy, ▶
woodsy areas than in the city.

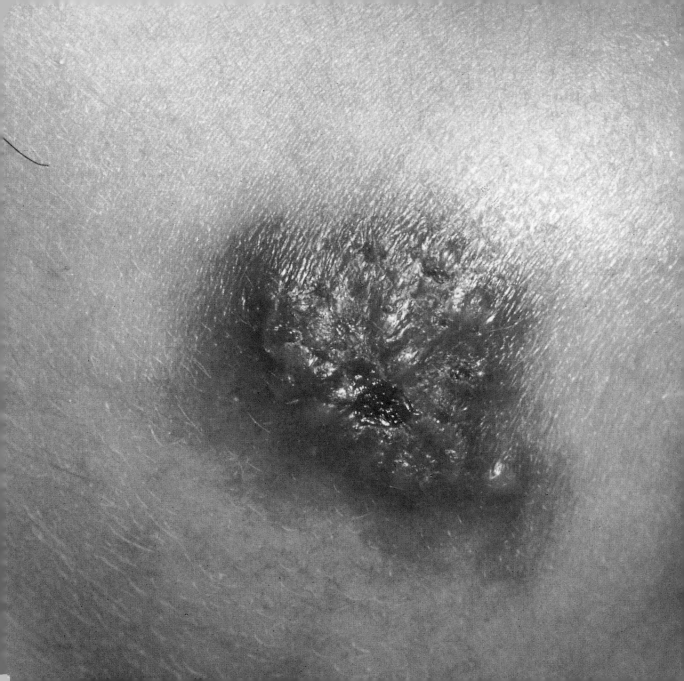

The Signs of Lyme Disease

If someone does get Lyme disease from a tick, he may get a **bull's-eye rash** (BULLS-eye RASH) first. This rash is usually in a pattern of a bull's-eye, with red circles around a patch of skin. Then the person may feel like he has the flu. He might have chills, headaches, or other body pains. After a while (maybe many months), the body pains could get very bad. It might become hard for him to move around.

◀ A rash from Lyme disease will look like a bull's-eye.

If You Feel Sick

It's not very easy to tell if someone has Lyme disease. People don't always get the bull's-eye rash. Sometimes they don't start to feel sick until months after getting a tick bite. And of course there are many reasons why someone might feel **achy** (AY-key). That's why it's important for you to tell your parents whenever you have a rash or feel sick. They will decide if you should see a doctor.

18

Be sure that you tell an adult ▶
if you feel achy or sick.

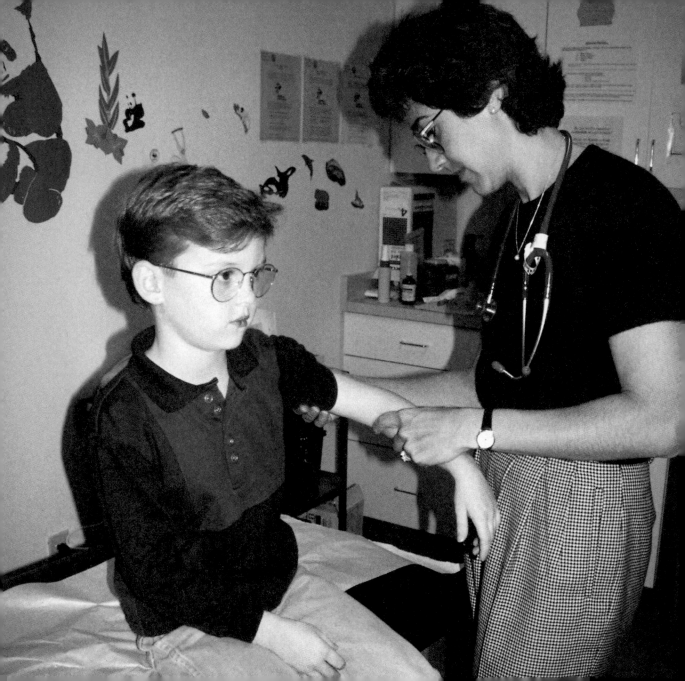

Your Doctor Can Help You

If you find a bull's-eye rash or have an achy feeling that won't go away, your parents will probably take you to the doctor. Your doctor will find out what's wrong. If you do have Lyme disease, you'll want to know as soon as you can. That way, your doctor can give you medicine that will help you get better.

◄ The doctor will be able to tell you if you have Lyme disease. Then she can help you if you do have it.

Know the Facts

Remember, a rash or soreness in your legs or arms does not usually mean that you have Lyme disease. Lyme disease is not a common illness, like chicken pox or the flu. Chances are, neither you nor your friends will ever get it. But now that you know the facts, you can protect yourself from ticks and get help if you think you may have been bitten by a tick.

Glossary

achy (AY-key) Sore.

bull's-eye rash (BULLS-eye RASH) A red area on your skin in a pattern of circles.

germ (JERM) Tiny living thing that can cause sickness.

Lyme disease (LIME diz-EEZ) An illness people can get from tick bites.

rash (RASH) A red or itchy area on your skin.

tweezers (TWEE-zerz) A small tool used for pulling things out of your skin.

Index

A
aches and pain, 17,
    18, 21
animals, 6, 9, 13,
    14

B
blood, 6

C
chills, 17
clothing, 13

D
doctor, 10, 18, 21

G
germs, 6, 10

grass, 6, 9, 13, 14

H
headaches, 17

L
Lyme disease, 5, 6
    getting, 14
    having, 17, 18, 21
    protection
        against, 13, 22

M
medicine, 21

P
pets, 9, 13

R
rash, 5, 22
    bull's-eye, 17, 18,
        21

T
ticks, 6, 9, 14, 17,
    18, 22
    protection against,
        13
    removing, 10

W
woods, 6